DISCOVER

Courtesy

Educational Assessment Publishing Company, Inc.

San Diego

Note to the Family

The **DISCOVER** book *Courtesy* is organized around key concepts that are essential for helping children develop courteous behavior. Each page presents high interest, colorful illustrations that assist children in understanding the concept of courtesy. The content uses age-appropriate language that is necessary for young children to comprehend and retain the book's main ideas.

In addition to the colorful illustrations and the easy-to-understand language, a question introduces each key concept. The use of the question helps the child and the parent focus on the main idea. By reading the question, the parent can initiate a discussion to discover the child's understanding of a concept and to clarify family values before or after reading the pages to the child.

The early sections of the book describe and define courtesy. These parts of the book help children understand the concept. In the later sections of the book, children apply the concept to realistic situations in which being courteous makes a difference. This strategy helps children and parents discuss courtesy in terms of the child's home life, school life, and relationships.

Reviewers

The publisher wishes to thank the following reviewers of **DISCOVER** for their valuable comments. They provided specific comments on the content, organization, and difficulty level of the material. Their assistance has been invaluable in creating a book that will be usable and profitable for parents and children.

Susan A. Burgess, MAT
Consultant, Children's Literature
Westwood, MA

Bruce Frazee, Ed.D.
Associate Professor
Trinity University
San Antonio, TX

Eileen McWhirter McNabb
Former Region Administrator
Los Angeles Unified School District
Los Angeles, CA

Editorial, design, and production by Book Production Systems, Inc.
Illustrations by Jane Barton Cover illustration by Stephanie Pershing.

1 2 3 4 5 6 7 8 9 — 96 95 94 93 92 91 90 89   ISBN 0-942277-62-7

Table of Contents

Introduction

Having courtesy means being considerate of others. A courteous person is someone who is thoughtful and kind. You feel good about yourself when you are courteous. And others are more likely to enjoy being around you.

What Is Courtesy?

Being courteous means being kind and considerate.
A considerate person thinks about others.

Being courteous means being thoughtful of others' rights and feelings.

Being courteous helps you get along with others.

Being courteous sometimes means thinking of others' needs before your own.

How Can You Show Courtesy?

You can show courtesy by saying polite words such as "thank you," "please," and "May I?".

You can show courtesy by offering to help with a chore or by opening a door for someone.

You can be courteous when you smile often . . .

and when you tell people that they have done
something well.

You can be courteous by listening to others.
Listening shows respect for the rights of others.

When you listen, you show that the other person is important.

How Does Being Courteous Show That You Are A Good Friend?

Being courteous to friends tells them you care about them.

When you are courteous, you are saying, "I like you."

Showing courtesy is a way to help others feel good about themselves.

People like to be around others who help them feel good.

What Might Happen If You Were Not Courteous?

If you did not listen to others, you might hurt their feelings.

If you were not thoughtful of others, getting along could be difficult.

If you were not courteous, others might not want to be around you.

If you do not show respect for others, they may not show respect for you.

How Does Being Courteous Make You Feel?

When you are courteous, you feel good about yourself.

It is easier to make friends. That makes you feel good.

Each person has a need for other people. Each person
has a need to belong and to be loved.

Being courteous helps you get along with others.
It helps you feel that you belong.

Aa Bb Cc Dd Ee Ff Gg Hh Ii Jj Kk
COURTESY
Please...
May I...
1.
2.
3.
4.
5.
6.
Thank you...
Would you...
This Mont
SUN MON TUES WED TH

Review

Showing courtesy is important. A courteous person is someone who is thoughtful and kind. A courteous person is easy to get along with. Each person has a need to belong, and being courteous helps you make friends. When you show courtesy, you will feel good about yourself. And others will feel good about you too!

Note to the Family

The next two pages contain vocabulary and
interactive activities that provide practice with
the important words and ideas just learned.
You can work with your child to reinforce these
concepts.

Fit the Words

Write the words that
fit the shapes. Use the
Word Bank for help.

belong
considerate
courtesy
thoughtful
listening

1. A courteous person is
   and kind.

2. A   person thinks
   about others.

3. You can show   by offering
   to help with a chore.

4.   shows respect for the rights
   of others.

5. Each person has a need to
   and to be loved.

You Can Show Courtesy

Next to each picture write how courtesy is being shown.

_____

_____

_____

_____

Please...

_____

_____

_____

_____

Write some ways you show courtesy to others.

_____

_____

_____

_____

Write some ways others have shown courtesy to you.

_____

_____

_____

_____